UH! OH! Jewish Holidays

Hidden Objects You'll (Almost) Never Find

Illustrated by Janet Zwebner

Yellow Brick Road
PRESS Ltd.

INTRODUCTION

*In this book, every illustration tells a story. Take a careful look at each picture and find the character in trouble -- the one who says the words "**UH! OH!**"*

*Then look in the box in the corner of each illustration. Besides the **UH! OH!**, there are four more objects for you to find. They are all hidden somewhere in the picture.*

Of course each picture tells you about one of the Jewish Holidays. You remember why we celebrate these Holidays, don't you?

*Did you say **UH! OH!**? Well, here are some clues to help you....*

ROSH HASHANAH

The Jewish New Year begins in the fall, about the time you start school. Apples are dipped in honey to signify the hope for a sweet year. Pomegranates are eaten because they are said to have 613 seeds, the exact number of commandments given to the Jewish people. Before Rosh Hashanah, some people wave a live chicken over their heads. This symbolizes their sincere wish to get rid of their bad deeds by transferring them to some other object, like a chicken. The chicken is then given as a gift to the poor so they can have food for the holidays. Less adventurous types may prefer to perform this custom by waving coins over their heads and then giving that money to help the poor. (The chickens probably like that better, too.)

Ten days after Rosh Hashanah, Jews begin a 24 hour fast to mark the holiest day of the year, Yom Kippur. Most of the day is spent in synagogue in prayer. It is a day when we ask God, and each other, for forgiveness for any wrongdoing we may have committed.

SUKKOT

Fifteen days after Rosh Hashanah, Jews build booths called Sukkot to remind them that the ancient Israelites camped in booths in the desert after they left Egypt over four thousand years ago. On Sukkot we hold an Etrog (a sweet smelling yellow fruit that looks like a lemon) in one hand, and a palm branch (lulav) tied together with myrtle (haddasim) and willow branches (arravot) in the other. Right after the last day of the week-long holiday of Sukkot we celebrate Simchat Torah. It is a special occasion because after reading a portion of the Bible every week for the entire year, we officially complete the Five Books of Moses. What next? Wave flags, eat jelly apples, and start reading all over again.

HANUKKAH

It was five brothers, and their father Mattityahu, who led the Jewish people in their rebellion against the evil Syrian Empire. This family, known as the Maccabees, persuaded the nation that even though they were few in number, they could stand up against their enemy and preserve their belief in one God. The Maccabees won battle after battle and chased the Greeks out of Israel. But, after the Jews returned to the Temple in Jerusalem, they found it full of idols. They wanted to light the giant Menorah right away, but there was not enough pure oil to fill its branches. One little jar of pure oil was found, and miraculously it lasted for eight days.

TU B'SHVAT

Trees and plants have their very own New Year, celebrated at the earliest hint of Spring, when the almond trees begin to blossom in Israel. Young Israeli Johnny Appleseeds plant new trees in farms and forests all over the country and Jews all over the world enjoy eating fruits that are harvested in Israel. If you live outside of Israel you can sponsor the planting of a tree; even have your name on it. But, as you'll see, it may pose some problems...

PURIM

The word "purim" means lottery. In ancient Persia an evil advisor, Haman, told King Ahashverosh to hold a lottery in order to choose a day on which to destroy all the Jewish people in the Kingdom. The King was almost ready to go along with Haman's plot, until Ahashverosh's wife, Queen Esther, intervened. Queen Esther, of course, was a Jewess. Her uncle, Mordechai, alerted her to the evil plot, and so Queen Esther was able to appeal to King Ahashverosh and save the Jewish people. Haman didn't make out too well. On Purim we twirl noisemakers, called groggers, as we listen to the story of Purim being recited out loud from the Scroll of Esther (Megillat Esther). Two important Purim traditions are the exchange of gifts of food between friends and helping the poor.

PASSOVER

"Why is this night different from all other nights?" is the question kids have asked at the Passover Seder for umpteen years. The answer is in the Passover Haggadah, the story of how we were rescued from Egypt; how Moses and Aaron warned Pharoh about the 10 plagues; and how he just wouldn't listen. We remember the magnificent way the sea parted so that the ancient Israelites could walk on dry land to freedom. We also remind ourselves that no man should be the slave of another.

ISRAEL INDEPENDENCE DAY

For many people, the Hebrew name for this holiday -- Yom Ha'atzmaut -- is a tongue twister. But if you like parades and flag waving, this is a holiday for you. Although Israel has been the Jewish homeland for thousands of years, it became an independent state again in May of 1948. It is a country that is ancient and brand new at the same time.

LAG B'OMER

Bonfires at night and picnics during the day are how Israelis celebrate this Holiday. In ancient times, when Torah study was forbidden by the Roman government, Rabbis and students managed to study the Torah by hiding in the fields. Lag B'Omer marks the end of a terrible plague in which over 20,000 great scholars and leaders of the Jewish people died. Yet, the fires of Torah learning continued to burn brightly.

SHAVUOT

Shavuot is celebrated precisely seven weeks after Passover. On Shavuot, God gave the Torah to the Jewish people who were huddled around Mount Sinai. Today, Jews eat milk products on this holiday as a reminder that on this day they became "officially" Jewish and could no longer use their non-kosher utensils. Shavuot also celebrates the bringing of the first fruits of the harvest to the Temple in Jerusalem.

On Shavuot we read the Book of Ruth in the synagogue. It tells the story of Ruth, a young woman from the land of Moab, who felt such a deep loyalty to the Jewish people that she converted and settled in the Land of Israel. Ruth was the grandmother of King David.

JERUSALEM DAY

Jerusalem was unified on June 7, 1967. When Israeli soldiers entered the Old City, it was announced with great emotion, "The Kotel is in our hands!" The Kotel is the outer Western Wall of the Ancient Jewish Temple. After the entire city of Jerusalem came back into Israeli hands as a result of the Six-Day War, Jews from all over the world streamed into the Old City.

It's true, some of the **UH! OH!** characters inside this book are pretty easy to find.

But watch out! Only 7 out of 10 kids tested between the ages of 8-12 were able to find all the **UH! OH!** Jewish Holidays characters, and the four hidden objects in each picture, within one hour.

If you can find the **UH! OH!** character and the four hidden objects in each picture within one hour, just fill out the form on the last page of this book and we'll make you an official **UH! OH!** TESTER.

You'll receive a sneak preview of our next **UH! OH!** title and get a chance to test your skills against our **UH! OH!** artists and writers.

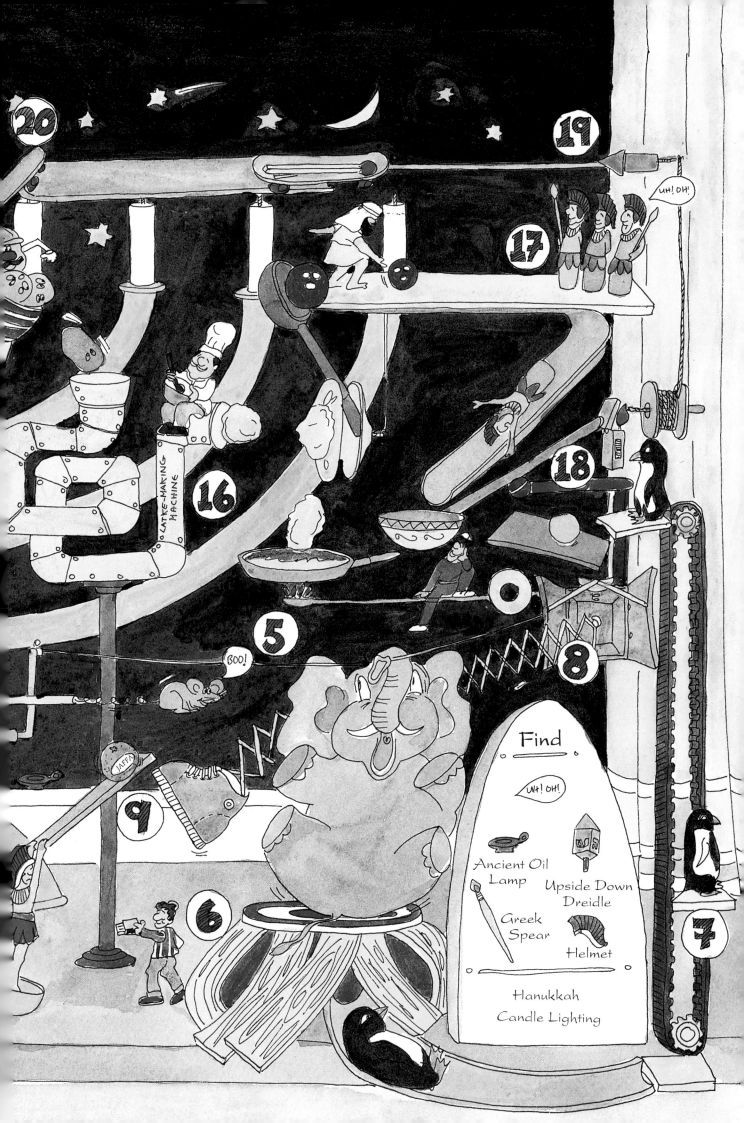

LOG TOSSING CONTEST

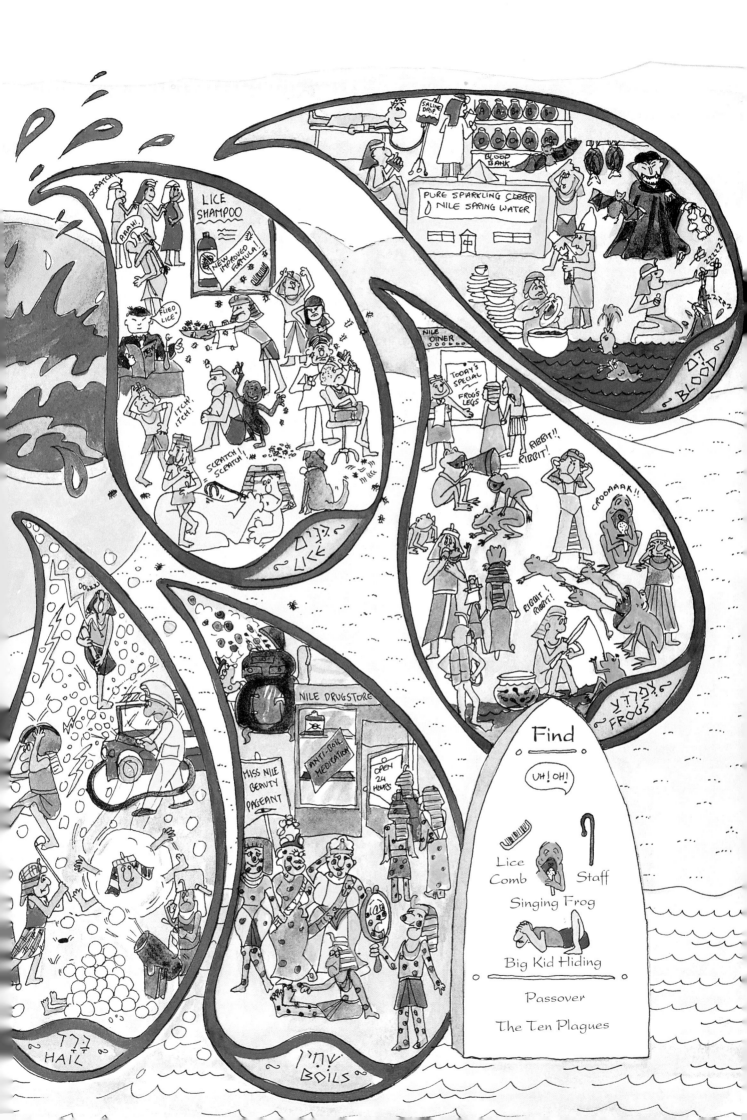

THE UH! OH! 1 HOUR TEST

How Well Did You Do?

TIME

Me	_____
Mom	_____
Dad	_____
Brother	_____
Sister	_____
Friend	_____

If you found all of the **UH! OH!** Jewish Holidays characters and the four hidden objects in each picture within 1 hour, then you qualify as an **UH! OH!** TESTER. Send in your Name, Address (city, state, zip) and Time to:

UH! OH! TESTER
POB 101
Woodmere, New York 11598

You'll receive a sneak preview of our next **UH! OH!** title and get a chance to test your skills against our **UH! OH!** artists and writers.